THE GRACE OF ZEN

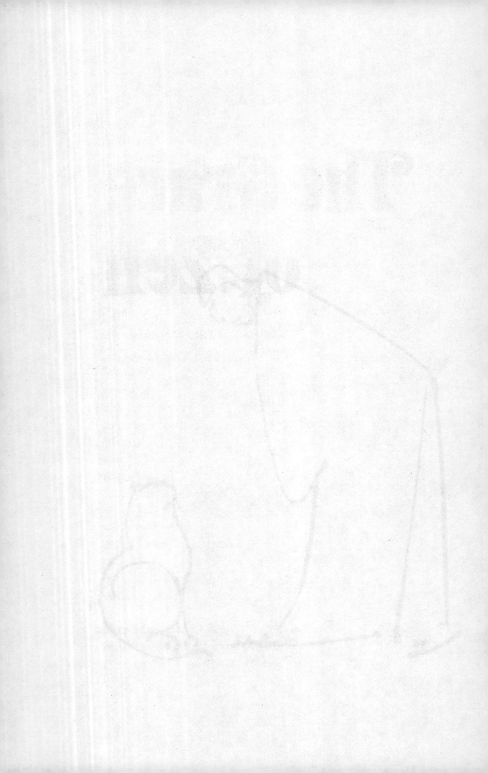

The Grace of Zen

Zen Texts for Meditation by

Ito Tenzaa Chuya
Dogen
Basho
Oemaru
Bunan
Musashi
Hakuin
Yoka Daishi
and others

Introduced by
Karlfried Durckheim

With a Preface by
Dom Aelred Graham

A Crossroad Book
The Seabury Press New York

The Seabury Press
815 Second Avenue
New York, N.Y. 10017

This translation and arrangement
copyright © Search Press Limited 1976

Translation by John Maxwell

Library of Congress Catalog Card Number: 76-52584
ISBN: 0-8164-2151-X (pbk.)

Printed in Great Britain

Contents

Preface

At first sight the title of this book might mislead the Western, and particularly the Christian, reader; but only at first sight. Grace in the sense of help from outside oneself would hardly apply, yet grace abounds — as mercy, kindness, charm, attractiveness. All these qualities are here exhibited, along with the robustness and challenge to self-examination, which characterize Zen.

Zen, as almost everyone now knows, means meditation — not as pondering on a theme but as direct insight into the reality of things. The word is Japanese but what the word stands for is Buddhist. This fact needs emphasizing, as Zen is often linked with a form of dilettante aestheticism, or in contrast, with the militarism of the samurai tradition, of which there is some evidence in these pages. No harm in that, as Zen excludes nothing except the false and unreal; it can blend with, even enliven, as has been shown, catholic Christianity.

Buddhism began in India with the teaching of Gautama, the 'all-enlightened one' (560 - 480 BC). It passed through Tibet and China where it was influenced by Confucianism, and more deeply by Taoism, before it took, among other Buddhist schools, the form of Zen in Japan, being a direct transmission from China. Zen's origins need noting if it is not to be misunderstood. Superficially it has little use for logical reasoning or the easily intelligible use of words. This is because the ultimate insight, as is well understood in the Indian tradition, cannot be expressed. Just as a Christian is unable to say adequately, or can best say only negatively, what he means by God, so the Zen *satori* experience is indescribable.

The reader should keep this in mind when he is confronted by these sometimes puzzling texts. Some are quite straightforward; others, poems and parables, often beautiful and always significant, are enigmatic and paradoxical, but repaying all the attention given to them; they are suggestive, allusive, pointing beyond themselves. A reader new to Zen might begin with the short passage from Dogen on page 9 (remembering that Za Zen means sitting meditation); then the celebrated highly thought-provoking comment of the future Sixth Patriarch on the words of a fellow pupil of his predecessor, on page 45; then he can take note, page 48, that there is nothing in the least fancy about Zen. After that, or before that (it hardly matters) he — meaning also, of course, she — can dip into the book at random and linger over its many half-hidden, somewhat Alice-in-Wonderland (including pictures), treasures.

The historic movement of Zen Buddhism has been from West to East — from India, through China and Korea, to America and Europe. This could have some significance for our times. In concrete terms Buddhism aims at producing a personality endowed with the fullest measure of understanding, compassion and selflessness. In this respect we find harmony rather than conflict with Christianity. The way is open to a wider ecumenism than is normally discussed among Church people. Hence the timeliness and importance of this book.

Aelred Graham

Ampleforth Abbey, York

To the reader

Zen texts are especially demanding. The closer you get to what lies behind the imagery, the more questions they raise. The more profound one's scrutiny, the more complex the conundrums they pose. Yet everything can suddenly become simple and lucid. That extraordinary directness and simplicity can often prove stimulating. Even someone unacquainted with the higher reaches of Zen can win from an image, word or sentence an unexpected impetus to laughter which paradoxically turns at once to contemplation. Equally he may find a certain resolution, or just as easily the strange burden of a responsibility which he had previously been unaware of but now all at once rises unquenchably in him.

Authentic Zen texts allow Life to speak directly. Not the everyday life of our continual round, but the Life that we are fundamentally; the Life we ought to live outwardly, but which makes no appearance in our conscious mind or in our conscience. Basically, then, a Zen text often means something other than what we read into it at first sight. Every Zen pronouncement is a parable. But what is referred to is always the Life that lies beyond life and death, and — most important of all — beyond all the dualisms into which the natural I (which likes to 'fix' everything it experiences) splits life. Authentic Life will not endure being fixed in concepts. But it can certainly be made to resound through the medium of a word, or to shine forth through an image; provided that the right eye is there to see it and the right ear to hear it.

3

But what are the right eye and ear? When are the eye and the ear wrong? When they are incapable of seeing and of hearing what it is all really about? They are always incompetent if they are mere organs of the world-ego, whose spiritual horizon extends no further than its inherited notions of the true, the good and the beautiful allow. Zen does not refer to a 'perfection' whose behaviour impeccably fulfils a preordained order of values. Zen is instead the place where the truth of effervescent life breaks forth, in an orderliness, fulness and power which put all preconceived ideals in the shade. Anyone who thinks that only what he can grasp is real, and that only what corresponds to traditional values is truly binding, will always find Zen disconcerting. Of course human life demands permanent laws and fixtures. But it ossifies wherever the *status quo*, which ensures the order of what has come to be, takes control. The point of all rationality is to provide space for the non-rational to flourish. The meaning of all order is to serve the generations of sentient beings. In the very moment in which calcified attitudes and thought-categories are shattered, Life that is beyond all orders and fixtures can illuminate the human consciousness. The Masters of Zen have an unfailing talent for the art of inducing such moments.

Whenever it is a question of real Life, of its expressions in action and creation, then the conventional operation of mind by which one logically confronts an object, a man or a 'text', retires in favour of a form of awareness in which one grasps the thing experienced not objectively but inwardly. Therefore an objective and rational approach to Zen texts is pointless. One has to engage with them in a wholly personal way and repeatedly to allow what is said to enter within one's self and quietly to take effect on one. Only what falls into

4

us as if into an empty bowl can come to anything, and produce its ever-widening circles like a stone dropped into motionless, unresisting water. Then the seed which a Zen text bears can grow as an increasingly profound question, a driving impulse, a new conscience, affirmative happiness, a fierce pain, a liberating comedy. But there is never a 'solution' which finally calms all unease, an ultimate knowledge one has certainly acquired and can as it were take home as a secure possession. One never possesses the content of a Zen text, unless as a thorn in the flesh goading one relentlessly onwards, ever deeper into the process of profound transformation.

Karlfried Dürckheim

Mountain bell

Blue mountain underfoot
White cloud overhead
Suddenly a temple bell booming
So loud it must be near at hand
But the mist so thick
How can I find it?
How can I know that it is?

Anon.

The arrow

We should not study Buddhism for our own sakes, nor practise it for honour or profit; we should not practise Za Zen in order to win merit, for an end; we should practise Za Zen for the sake of Za Zen. That is the true way, that is true Zen. If we 'want' a result, it will last only a short time; just as the arrow eventually returns to earth, it will soon be at an end. Za Zen is good for health, for the culture of the spirit, but when we practise Za Zen we should not think of the effect.

Dogen

We are more than self

Behind a temple stood a field in which pumpkins were growing. One day the pumpkins fell to quarrelling. The heads divided into two parties, made an unholy row and insulted one another fiercely. The good monk who had charge of the temple heard the vulgar brawling and ran out to see what could be the matter. He discovered the pumpkins raging at one another and upbraided them: 'Pumpkins, you must be insane to attack one another like this! Start practising Za Zen this minute!' The pious monk showed the pumpkins how to practise Za Zen: 'Cross your legs, sit there with a straight back!'

The pumpkins did as they were told and while they were practising Za Zen their anger subsided. Then, as peace reigned, the Master said: 'Everyone now put his hand on his head!' They did so, and every pumpkin felt something extraordinary happening up there above him. They all found that a living runner went from one to the other, joining them together, and making them one plant. Ashamed of their previous conduct, they declared: 'How very strange. We are all joined together and all of us live one life together. And yet we went quite mad and started fighting one another. How stupid we were! Our good monk is quite right!' And since then the whole colony of pumpkins has lived in peace and amity.

An Edo parable

Reversal

Moon unchanged,
Unchanged flowers.
I, however, am now
The thingness of things seen.

Bunan

Hot and cold

Below, the town summer-hot
Above, Mount Koma snow-thick
Thus the life of Zen
The lotus withstands earth-fire.

Tokuo

Every man is Buddha

Men are Buddha in their deepest being
As water is ice. And just as there is no ice without
Water so there is no man without Buddha.
Alas for those who seek afar off
And do not know what lies close at hand!
They are like those who stand up to their waists
in water
And continue to shout for water.
They are heirs of rich and noble families
yet they fall into poverty and suffering.

Hakuin

13

Fellow feeling

Lying sick
In my life's black winter
Only now I ask after my neighbour.

Basho

Subversion

The Lord Mihara decided one day that he needed a new painting. He summoned a competent man, gave him the commission, and some weeks later the painter turned up with his picture. It was a wild goose. When he saw the painting Mihara flew into a rage. In the natural order, wild geese fly side by side. That picture is subversive! Mihara's courtiers found the situation unbearable and went to see Zen Master Motsugai. Lord Mihara was very fond of Motsugai who was clever and tough. He could punch through a wooden board (he was called 'Puncher Bonze'). He was a good spear man and a first-class rider. But he was also a sage and a fine calligrapher. Motsugai hurried off to see Mihara. He merely glanced at the painting and then wrote this above the bird: 'The first wild goose! One after the other in never-ending line!' That put the Lord Mihara into a good mood again and he rewarded the painter and Master Motsugai most handsomely.

Anon.

Universal garment

Universal garment, unending and blessed.
Now I have the satori of Buddha
I can help all beings.
O wonderful freedom!

Sutra of Master Nyojo

The duties of a Samurai

1. Do not criticize moral and social traditions.
2. Do not lead a life of personal desire.
3. Think little of yourself.
4. Think much of others.
5. Do not desire much in your life.
6. Do not regret much in regard to yourself.
7. Do not envy others their success.
8. Do not regret parting.
9. Do not harbour resentment against others.
10. Do not love too deeply.
11. Do not hate.
12. Do not build houses which are too beautiful or too big.
13. Do not eat too much, or too rich foods.
14. Do not possess many changes of clothing; do not wear fine garments or jewels.
15. Do not be superstitious.
16. Do not spend money on anything other than your sword.
17. Do not fear death in the service of your master or in order to help another.
18. Do not possess too much money.
19. Respect the Buddha and the gods but do not pray to them or depend on them.
20. Uphold honour without fearing death.
21. Never forget the way of the Samurai.

Miyamoto Musashi

The marvellous cat

by Zen-Master Ito Tenzaa Chuya

An exemplary tale from an ancient Japanese school of combat, translated from the Japanese by Takeharu Teramoto and Fumio Hashimoto and adapted by Karlfried Dürckheim*

Once upon a time there was a Master of combat called Shoken. His house was plagued by a big rat. It ran about even in broad daylight. One day Shoken shut the room door and gave the household cat an opportunity to catch the rat. But the rat flew at the cat's face and gave it such a sharp bite that it ran off screeching. Evidently the creature couldn't be got rid of so easily. So the master of the house collected together a number of cats that had won a fair reputation in the neighbourhood and let them into the room. The rat hunched itself up in a corner. As soon as a cat approached it, it bit the cat and scared it off.

The rat looked so nasty that none of the cats dared to take it on a second time. That put Shoken into a

* I am indebted for this text to my Zen Master, Takeharu Teramoto. Teramoto was an Admiral and Professor at the Naval Academy in Tokyo. His form of practice was sword fighting (*Gyo*). His own Master had been the last Master of a school of combat in which the story of five cats had been handed down from Master to Master since the beginning of the seventeenth century as a form of instruction, and had finally reached Teramoto through his own Master.

20

perfect rage. He went after the rat himself, determined to kill it. But the wily beast escaped every blow and feint from the experienced Master; he just couldn't wear it down. In his attempts to do so, he split doors, *shojis, karakamis,* and so forth. But the rat flashed through the air like lightning, jumped up at his face, and bit the Master. At last, running with sweat, he called out to his servant 'They say that six to seven *cho* from here there is the toughest and cleverest cat in the world. Bring it here!'.

The servant brought the cat. It didn't look so very different from other cats. It didn't look particularly sharp or bright. So Shoken didn't expect anything special from it. But he thought he would try it all the same, so he opened the door and let it into the room. The cat entered very softly and slowly as if it was expecting nothing out of the ordinary. But the rat recoiled then stayed motionless. So the cat approached it slowly and deliberately and carried it out in its mouth.

That evening the defeated cats met in Shoken's house, respectfully accorded the old cat the place of honour, paid it homage and said humbly: 'We are all supposed to be highly efficient. We have all practised and sharpened our claws in order to defeat all kinds of rats, and even weasels and otters. We had never suspected that there could be a rat as strong as that one. But tell us, what art did you use to vanquish it so easily? Do not keep your art a secret. Let us into the mystery.' The old cat laughed, and said: 'You young cats are indeed efficient. But you don't know the right way to go about things. And so when something unexpected happens you're unsuccessful. But first tell me how you have practised'.

A black cat came out to the front and said: 'I come from a line of celebrated rat-catchers. I too decided to

21

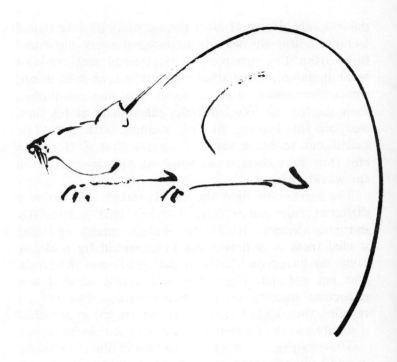

become one. I can jump over screens two metres high; I can force myself through a tiny hole that only rats can negotiate. From the time I was a kitten I have practised all the acrobatic arts. Even when I wake up and I still haven't quite come to, and I see a rat scampering across the balcony, I get it straightaway. But that rat today was stronger and I suffered the most frightful defeat that I have ever experienced in my whole life. I have been put to shame'. Then the old cat said: 'What you have practised is only technique (*shosa* – sheer physical skill). But your spirit is pre-occupied with the question: How am I to win? And that problem is still consuming you when you reach the target! When the ancient Masters taught "technique", they did so in order to show

22

their pupils a "means of the way" (*michisuyi*). Their technique was simple yet contained the highest truth. But posterity has been preoccupied with technique and technique alone. In that way much has been discovered, but all according to the rule: If you do *this* or *that*, then this or that will happen. But what does happen? No more than dexterity — skill pure and simple. The traditional way has been abandoned; much ingenuity has been applied to an exhaustive pitting of technique against technique, until we have indeed reached the point of exhaustion. We can go no further. That always happens when people think of technique and success and put no more than ingenuity into play. Ingenuity — cleverness — is however a function of the spirit; if it is not based on the Way and aims only at perfect skill, then it falls victim to error and what has been achieved is lost. Think about this and practise from now on in the right spirit'.

At that a big tabby-cat came forward and said: 'In the art of fighting it is a matter of the spirit, and it must always be so. Therefore I have always practised strength of spirit (*ki wo neru*). As far as I am concerned, my spirit always seems as hard as steel and free and charged with the presence of the Spirit that fills heaven and earth (Mencius). As soon as I see an enemy, he is already vanquished; no sooner do I see him than he is thrall to that mighty Spirit and I have already won the battle in advance. Only then do I advance! I do so quite instinctively, as the situation demands. I move according to the 'feel' of my opponent; I take the rat from the right or the left as I wish and I anticipate my adversary's every move. I never worry about technique as such. It happens of its own accord. If a rat runs across the balcony, I have only to stare at it for it to fall into my clutches. But the rat of which we are speaking comes

23

without shape or form and goes without leaving any trace. What does that mean? I cannot say'. Then the old cat remarked: 'What you have been concerned with is of course the effect of that great Power that fills heaven and earth. But what you have actually achieved is only a mental power and not that good power which serves the name of Good. The very fact that you are conscious of the power with which you intend to conquer prevents your victory. Your ego is in question. But what if your adversary's ego is stronger than your own? When you try to overcome the enemy with the superior force of your own power, he pits his own power against yours. Do you imagine that you alone can be strong and that all others must be weak? The real question is how to behave when there is something that in spite of all one's willing one cannot defeat with the superior weight of one's own power. What you experience as "free" and "tempered" and "filling heaven and earth" within you is not the great Power itself (*ki no sho*), but only its reflection in you. It is your own spirit, and therefore but a shadow of the great Spirit. It appears to be the great power, but in reality it is something quite different. The Spirit of which Mencius speaks is strong because it is permanently illumined by great understanding. But your spirit obtains its power only under certain conditions. Your power and that of which Mencius speaks have different origins. They are as different from one another as the eternal flow of a river, for instance the Yangtse Kiang, is from a sudden downpour one night. But what is the spirit that one should rely on when faced with an enemy who cannot be conquered with any mere restricted mental power (*kisei*)? That is the real question! There is a proverb which says: "A rat in the trap will even bite the cat." If the enemy is in the jaws of death he has no resources to depend on. He forgets his life; he forgets all need; he forgets himself; he is beyond victory and defeat. And thus his will is tempered like steel. How could one conquer him with a spiritual power which one ascribes to oneself alone?'

Then an ageing grey cat came slowly forward and said: 'Yes, it is indeed as you say. Mental power whatever its strength has a form (*katachi*) in itself. But whatever has form, however small it may be, can be grasped. Therefore I have for a long time trained my soul (*kokoro*, the power of the heart). I do not practise the power which overcomes others spiritually ('*sei*', like the second cat). And I do not hit out round about me (like the first cat). I reconcile myself with my opponent, get onto equal terms with him, and do not oppose him in any way. If the other is stronger than I am, then I simply acknowledge that, and so to speak give into his will. My art is rather to gather the flying pebbles in a loose cloth. A rat that tries to attack me may be as strong as you like, but it will find nothing to fly against, nothing to get to grips with. But today's rat simply didn't respond to my trick. It came and went as mysteriously as God himself. I have never encountered one like it'.

Then the old cat said: 'What you call propitiation does not arise from being, from the Greatness of Nature. It is an artificial, botched-up reconciliation - a mere artifice. Your conscious intention is to elude the adversary's spirit of attack. But because you are thinking about it, however fleetingly, he realizes what your plan is. If you try to conciliate him, with a spirit thus composed, then your spirit (in so far as it concentrates on the attack) will be confused, mixed-up, and your sharpness of perception and action will be considerably reduced. Whatever you do with fully conscious intent

25

restricts the original pulsation of the Greatness of Nature as it takes effect from the depths of Mystery; it upsets the flow of your spontaneous movement. How then are you to put a miraculous power into practice? Only when you think of nothing, and do nothing, and in your movement surrender yourself to the pulsation of Being (*shizen no ka*), will you have lost all tangible form, and be so that nothing on earth can act as a counter-form; then there is no enemy left to resist you.

'I do not believe that everything that you have practised is pointless. Everything can be a means of the way. Technique and Tao can be one and the same, and then the great Spirit, the 'governing Spirit', is already incorporated in you and is revealed in the action of your body. The power of the great Spirit (*ki*) serves the human person (*ishi*). He who has free access to *ki* can encounter everything within infinite freedom and in the right way. If his spirit is reconciled, it will not shatter even on gold or rock, and need exert no special power in battle. Only one thing is necessary: that no trace of egotism - of I-consciousness - comes into play, lest everything should be lost. If you think about all that, however fleetingly, then all will be artificial. It will not arise from Being, from the original pulsation of the body of the Way (*do-tai*). Then the adversary will not submit to you but resist in his own behalf. What sort of a way or art is to be used? Only when you are in that disposition which is free of all consciousness of self, when you act without acting, without intention and stratagem, in unison with the Greatness of Nature, are you on the right Way. Abandon all intent, practise purposelessness and let it happen simply out of Being. This way is unending, inexhaustible'.

26

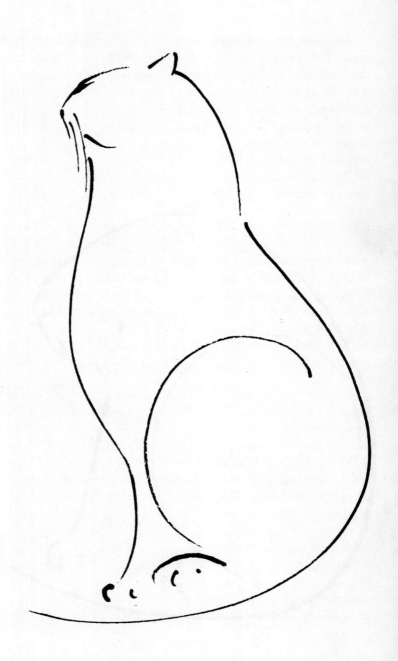

And the old cat added something astounding: 'You must not believe that what I have told you today is the highest of things. Not long ago a certain tom-cat was living in the next village to me. He slept the whole day long. No trace of anything resembling spiritual power was to be observed in him. He just lay there like a lump of wood. No one had ever seen him catch a rat. But wherever he was, there wasn't a rat to be seen! And wherever he popped up or laid himself down, no rat ever appeared. One day I looked up and asked what that meant. He did not answer me. I asked him another three times. He was silent. But that doesn't mean that he didn't want to reply. Instead he clearly didn't know what he should say. But that is how it is: "He who knows says nothing, and he who says it knows it not". The cat had forgotten himself and everything round-about him. He had become "nothing". He had reached the highest level of purposelessness. We can say that he had found the way of divine knighthood, which is to vanquish without killing. I am still a long way behind him'.

Shoken heard all this as if in a dream, came by, greeted the old cat and said: 'For a long time now I have been practising the art of fighting, but I have not yet reached the end. I have absorbed your insights and I think that I have understood the true meaning of my way, but I ask you earnestly to tell me something more about your craft'. The old cat replied: 'How is that possible? I am only an animal and the rat is my food. How should I know about human affairs. All I know is this: the meaning of the art of combat is not merely a matter of vanquishing one's opponent. It is rather an art by which at a given time one enters into the great clarity of the primal light of death and life (*seishi wo akiraki ni suru*). In the midst of all his technical practice

29

a true Samurai should always practise the spiritual acquisition of that clarity of mind. For that purpose however he must plumb before all else the teaching of the ground of being of life and death, and the teaching of the order of death (*shi no ri*). But only he acquires great clarity of mind who is free from everything which could lead him off that way (*hen kyoku*). When Being and encounter with Being (*shin ki*) are left undisturbed, to themselves, free from the ego and from all things, then whenever it is appropriate it can declare its presence in complete freedom. But if your heart even fleetingly attaches itself to something, then Being itself is attached and is turned into something arrested in itself. But if it becomes something arrested in itself, then there is something there that resists the I that is in itself. Then two entities face one another and fight one another for dominance. If that happens then the miraculous functions of being, even though used to all change, are restricted, the jaws of death gape close, and that clarity of perception proper to Being is lost. How then is it possible to meet the adversary in the right frame and peacefully contemplate 'victory and defeat'? Even if you win, you win no more than blind victory that has nothing to do with the spirit of the true art of combat.

'Being free from all things does not of course mean an empty void. Being as such has no nature in itself. In and for itself it is beyond all form. It stores up nothing in itself. But if one grasps and remembers even fleetingly what it is and how fragile it is, the great Power will cling to it and it will contain the equilibrium of forces that flows from the Source. But if Being is even slightly subject to or imprisoned by something, it is no longer able to move freely and cannot pour forth in all its fulness. If the equilibrium that eman-

30

ates from Being is disturbed, if its power is at all apparent it quickly overflows; but without power its balance is inadequate. Where it overflows, too much power breaks out and there is no holding it back. Where it is inadequate, the active spirit is weakened and wanting and is never sufficient for the situation when it is called on.

'What I call freedom of things means only that if one does not lay up stores, one has nothing to rely on. Without secure provision there is no position to take up and nothing objective to have recourse to. There is neither an I nor an anti-I. When something comes along, one meets it as it were unawares, without any impact. In the *Eki* (the Book of Changes), it is written: "Without thinking, without action, without movement; quite still. Only thus can one proclaim the nature and law of things from within, quite unconsciously, and at last become one with heaven and earth". Whoever practises and understands the art of combat in that sense is close to the truth of the Way'.

When Shoken heard this, he asked: 'What does that mean, that neither a subject nor an object, neither an I nor an anti-I is there?' The cat answered: 'If and because an I is there, there is an enemy there. If we do not present ourselves as an I, then there is no opponent there. What we call opponent, adversary, enemy, is merely another name for what means opposition or counterpart. In so far as things maintain a form, they also presuppose a counter-form. But wherever something is present as *a* something, it has a specific form. If my being is not constituted as a specific form, then there is no counter-form there. Where there is no counterpart, no opposition, there is nothing which can come forth to oppose me. But that means that neither an I nor an anti-I is there. If one wholly abandons self and thus

31

becomes free, from the foundations upwards and from every thing, then one will be in harmony with the world and one with all things in the great universal oneness. Even when the enemy's form is extinguished one remains unconscious of it. That does not mean that one is wholly oblivious of it, but that one does not dwell upon it, and the spirit continues free from all attachment and even in its actions responds simply and freely from the centre of being. If the spirit is no longer possessed by anything and is free from all obsession, then the world, just as it is, is wholly our world and one with us. That means that henceforth one apprehends it beyond good and evil, beyond sympathy or antipathy. One is no longer caught up in anything and is no longer attached to anything in the world. All oppositions which present themselves to us, profit and loss, good and evil, joy and suffering, have their origin in us. Therefore in the whole spread of heaven and earth nothing is so worthy of discernment as our own being. An ancient poet said: "A speck of dust in one's eye and even the three worlds are still too narrow. If nothing matters to us any longer and is no longer of consequence to us, then the smallest bed is too wide for us." In other words, if a speck of dust enters our eye, the eye will not open; for we can see clearly only if there is nothing within, but now the dust has penetrated to obstruct the vision within. Similarly with being that shines forth as light and illumination, and is essentially free of everything that is "something". When however something does present itself, the very presentation destroys its essence. Another writer put it this way: "If one is surrounded by foes, by a hundred thousand enemies, one's form is so to speak pulverized. But my being, my nature, is mine and remains my own, however strong my enemy may be. No adversary can penetrate my being my self". Confucius said: "You cannot steal the being of even a simple man". But if the spirit is confused, then being will turn against us".

'That is all that I can tell. Now return to yourselves and know yourselves. A master can only teach his pupil the lesson and try to justify it. But "I myself" have to realize the truth and take it as my own. That is called self-appropriation (*jitoku*). It is transferred from heart to heart (*ishin denshin*). It is a bestowal by extraordinary means, beyond instruction and erudition (*kyogai betsuden*). That does not mean that the Master's teaching is to be contradicted. All it means is that even a Master cannot pass on the truth itself. That is not only true of Zen. From the spiritual exercises of the ancients on the art of forming the soul right up to the arts proper, self-appropriation is always the essence of the matter, and it is always transmitted from heart to heart, apart from tradition, from all teachings which are handed down. The meaning of all "teaching" is only to show what everyone possesses in himself without already knowing it, and then to make him aware of it. There is no secret that the master can "hand over" to the pupil. Teaching is easy. Listening is easy. But it is difficult to become aware of what one has in one's self, to mark it out and really to take possession of it. That is known as looking into one's own being. It is self-perception, the self-perception of being (*ken-sei, kensho*). If that happens to us then we have Satori. It is the great awakening out of the dream of errors. Awakening, looking into one's own being, perception of the self one really is — they are all one and the same thing'.

Reality

I am not sure
That reality is real.
That is why this world seems the world it is.
But if that is so, how dare I feel
That dreams are no more than dreams?

Saigyo

Calm

Hot night.
Half stripped,
A snail moon-bathes.

Issa

The story of Yoka

by Eno (the sixth Patriarch)

Yoka (Yoka Daishi) is the author of one of the most famous works on the Zen way to illumination, the Shodoka. The story of Yoka is taken from the Dan Kyo by Eno (Houei Neng), from whom he learnt the way of Zen meditation.

The Zen Master Genkaku (or deep Satori), Yoka Daishi, came from the village of Yoka. He was born into a Tai family in the state of On Shu. As a young student he applied himself to the sutras and shastras. He knew the teaching of Samatha (tranquillization) and Vipassana (profound insight). On reading the *Vimalakirti Nidesa Sutra* he reached an intuitive understanding of the mystery of his own spirit. In other words, he realized the essence of spirit.

Yoka had a friend called Gensaku, who was a pupil of the sixth Patriarch, Eno. He visited him and during their conversation he noted that Genkaku's commentaries agreed with what the various Patriarchs had said. So he asked him:

'What is the name of the Master who gave you Dharma?

'I was under instruction,' said Genkaku, 'when I studied the sutras and shastras of the Vaipulya order, but it was when I read the *Vimalakirti Nirdesa Sutra* that I realized the meaning of the Dhyana school (school of the Spirit of Buddha). In this respect I have not yet had a Master to confirm my understanding.'

'When the Buddhas of the past were alive', said Gensaku, 'it was possible to dispense with the services of a Master, but since then anyone who reaches illumination without the help and confirmation of a Master is necessarily a heretic.'

'Will you be my sponsor?' asked Genkaku.

'My words have no weight,' replied Gensaku. 'At Sokei you can meet the sixth Patriarch. People from all parts visit him seeking for Dharma. If you want to go, I shall be happy to take you there.'

When they reached Sokei for an interview with the Patriarch, Genkaku took three turns about him, then stood there without greeting Eno. The Patriarch noted Genkaku's rude behaviour and said:

'A Buddhist monk is the personification of three thousand precepts of morality and of eight thousand minor rules of discipline. Where are you from and what makes you so sure of yourself?'

'Since the question of eternal rebirth is an urgent problem and death can occur at any time, I have no time to waste on ceremony and I should like you to give me a direct answer to this problem.'

'Why do you not take the principle of "no birth" as an answer to the problem of the transience of life?' said the Patriarch.

'To realize the essence of spirit is to be free of birth,' answered Genkaku, 'and once that problem is resolved the question of transience no longer exists.'

'That is true, that is true,' said the Patriarch.

Without more ado Genkaku did homage to Eno according to the ceremonial of leavetaking.

'Aren't you leaving rather abruptly?' said the Patriarch.

'How can there be any such thing as swiftness, and therefore abruptness, if motion does not exist in itself?' asked Genkaku.

39

'Who knows that motion does not exist?' asked the Patriarch.

'I hope that you will not be more specific,' said Genkaku.

The Patriarch praised him for his full understanding of the idea of "no birth" but Genkaku retorted:

'Is there an idea of "no birth"?'

'How can one be specific without an idea?' aked the Patriarch.

'That which specifies is not an idea,' said Genkaku.

'Well answered!' said the patriarch. He then asked Genkaku to delay his leavetaking and to spend the night there. It was from then on that Genkaku was known to his contemporaries as the enlightened one who spent a night in the Patriarch's house.

The moon rises

The moon rises.
Leaf upon leaf upon leaf
Flutters down.

Shiki

Perception

Quick dragon-fly
Shiny wings gone —
Bright red pepper.

Kikaku

Bright red pepper
With shiny wings —
Quick dragon-fly.

Basho

42

Insults

A Brahmin visited the Buddha one day and insulted him
and Dharma. The Buddha said nothing for some time
and then spoke: 'Have you finished?' The Brahmin
said that he had no more to say. Then the Buddha said:
'If you had brought a gift and I had refused it, you
would have taken it away with you. It is the same with
your insults. You will take them away with you.'

The Sutra of Forty-two Articles

Unfettered mind

Untutored,
The bird comes and goes, plashing.
But the water is still.

Dogen

Buddha's tree

The body is the Buddha's tree.
The heart is like a brilliant mirror
Which we wipe and clean unceasingly
So that no dust clings to it.

> *Chen Sieou* (Pupil of the fifth Patriarch)

There is no tree of Buddha
No brilliant mirror
For essentially everything is empty.
Where then could the dust rest?

> *Eno* (Pupil of the fifth Patriarch,
> and then sixth Patriarch)

Dewdrop

Dewdrop, let me rinse
In your swift sweet water
The dark hands of life.

Basho

The treasure in our heart

Once upon a time there were two friends, one poor and one rich. The rich man invited the poor one to visit him. When he had drunk and eaten well his poor friend went to sleep. The rich man, pitying him greatly, slipped a diamond into his pocket and departed. But since the poor man did not know that he had a great treasure, he continued to lead his life of poverty, sometimes even begging to keep going. Some years later he happened to meet his rich friend, and asked him for alms. The rich man said: 'Why are you begging? Why are you still poor, when I gave you a jewel of great price?' Then the poor man felt in his pocket and found the diamond.

from the *Hoke Kyo*
(Saddharma Pundarika Sutra)

The true spirit of Buddha

Pupil: What is the true spirit of Buddha?

Master: The wall of the cloister, the walls of the house, the roof and the pathways.

Anon.

True Dharma

The true Dharma of Buddhism, which came from Buddha himself, was handed down by Mayakasyapa, Ananda, Nagarjuna and Bodhidharma. It is known as True Zen. There is an absolute, unique and supreme method of reaching Satori, which is the essence and expression of Dharma. This method is transmitted directly from my spirit to your spirit. You cannot learn from books or through the judgment of others since the method requires complete inward freedom. The practice of Za Zen is the main gateway to this inward freedom.

Dogen

Awakening

Sleeping butterfly
Delicate fold on temple gong —
The gong rang!

Buson

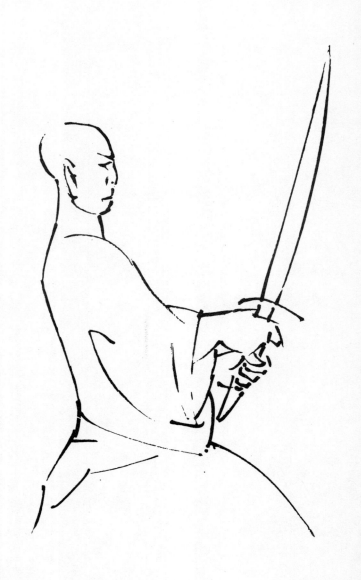

The void

Tesshu was a renowned sword fighter and Zen adept. He visited Dokuon and declared portentously that everything that existed was a pure void; that neither he nor Dokuon really existed but just imagined they were there. Master Dokuon said nothing while Tesshu preached away, but when he had finished he picked up his long smoker's pipe and gave Tesshu a smart blow on the head. Tesshu was so angry at this that he almost killed Dokuon and would in fact have done so if the Master had not said, quite unmoved: 'The void is very soon roused to anger, I see . . .' Tesshu smiled weakly and departed.

Anon.

Perseverance

Stubborn bird
Woodpecker at dusk
At the same spot.

Issa

Not-two

Believing is not-two
Not-two is belief in what
is inexpressible
Past and future
are surely an eternal
Now . . .

Shindin mei

The non-gate

The Zen school makes the spirit of Buddha's word the basis and the non-gate the gate of Dharma. But if there is only a non-gate how can one pass through? Do you not know the saying: 'What goes through the gate is not the treasure of the house'? ... How can one understand so long as one stays attached to words? The use of words is like striking out at the moon with a stick or scratching one's shoe because one's foot itches.

Wu-Men.

Unmoving

Walking is Zen
Sitting too is Zen.
If I talk or say nothing,
If I rest or hurry along,
In essence everything is
Unmoving.

Shodoka

Reflection

Every night the moon's
reflection is in the stream
But if you try to find the spot
where it touched the water
you cannot find even a shadow.

Takuan

The Shodoka of Yoka Daishi

The hymn of immediate satori,
stanzas 1 to 27; 32, 39, 54

1

Dear friend, do you see this true Zen Master?
He has forgotten the intellectual understanding of what
he has learnt in order to reach profound understanding.
Thus he practises easily and freely what he has learnt
and what he wants to learn.
He lives in equanimity, calm and content. He is free
from all care, and he acts naturally and reasonably.
He does not struggle to avoid illusion nor does he seek
for Satori.
He knows that illusion is unfounded and that Satori
is none other than himself.
He sees the real nature of not-knowing as the nature
of the Buddha and he sees that the reality of his illusory
body is equivalent to *Dharma Kaya*, the eternal body
of the Buddha.

2

When he fully realizes the Dharma Kaya, the body of Dharma, he has nothing.
He himself is the source of all things and his ordinary life is another name for the eternal Buddha.
The five skandas* come and go like clouds in the blue sky.
The spray of three poisons, covetousness, anger and ignorance, appears and disappears like a mirage above the ocean.

* The five elements of individuality: form; sensation; perception; that which forms and is formed; conscience.

3

When he realizes the suchness, the real nature of things
(*Jisso*), he is without illusion in regard to his personal
desires and his limited ideas.

He knows that there is no essential ego existing in him,
and he sees clearly the emptiness of all forms, as merely
a shadow in relation both to subjective and to objective elements.

If you live in Zen, you can change your Karma (process
of cause and effect; thoughts, words and physical actions
and their results) in a moment (*Setsuna*).

If I say anything which is untrue, may I fall into the
great hell* (*Avici*) or into the hell where they tear out
one's tongue.

* A spiritual state.

4

If you reach the Zen of Buddha*, at that very moment
You accomplish the six Paramita (*Roku do*) and the ten
thousand good actions.
In your dream there are six pathways (*Roku Shu*)
But when you wake up, they are reduced to nothing
Neither error, nor happiness, nor loss, nor gain.
Do not try to find them in the essence of spirit.
It is a long time since you wiped the dust from your
mirror
Now it is time for you to see its brilliancy perfectly.

* The highest form of Zen, beyond thinking and non-thinking,
simple posture, without goal. It is emptiness, the illumination
of the Buddha, true peace and freedom.

5

Who can not-think (*Mu Nen*) and what is non-existence
(*Mu Sho*)?
If there really is non-existence, there is no birth.
Ask a statue if it is happy
If you practise charity in crder to become Buddha
When will you succeed? Never, forever.

6

Do not deliver yourself up, do not clutch at the four elements* (*Shi Dai*)
Drink and eat according to your true nature
All things in the universe are impermanent (*Hu Jo*), and therefore all existence is void.
That is the whole understanding of Buddha.

* Earth, water, fire, air, which constitute all things and therefore our body.

7

A committed disciple of the Buddha speaks in accordance with the ultimate, the absolute truth.
If you do not agree with what I say you are free to discuss it.
Nevertheless, remember that Buddhism should cut the root and not the branches and the leaves.

8

Most people do not recognize the perfect jewel, the jewel of supreme wisdom, *Satori*.
It is hidden in the secret place of *Tathagata*, awaiting its discovery,
The six senses and the six worlds are interwoven, making life as it is.
Complete illusion, yet nothing exists which might be called illusion.
The perfect light of this jewel of wisdom enlightens humanity.
There is neither form nor colour any more than there is non-form or non-colour.

9

Elucidate the five kinds of visions* and acquire the
five powers.**
That is possible only by practising Za Zen
beyond speculation.
You can see clouds naturally in the mirror but
To hold on to the moon's reflection in water is
impossible.

* The fleshly eye, the vision of the ordinary man; the subtle,
divine vision which enables one to see the future of things; the
eye of wisdom by which emptiness can be perceived; the eye of
the law, of Dharma by which Bodhissattva see all those teachings
which enable them to lead men to enlightenment; the eye of
Buddha, total vision comprising the four preceding types.

** Faith or confidence; energy to proceed towards death; attention or memory; concentration and synthesis; supreme wisdom.

10

We must go alone and walk alone at all times.
Those who have reached the goal can play on the path
of Nirvana.
The old Zen Masters have natural, traditional manners
and are harmonious.
Their spirit is simple, clean, pure and sincere.
Just as their bearing is noble and dignified, simple and
harmonious, and they show no particular attraction,
no one pays them any special attention.

11

The sons of Sakya, the Buddha's true disciples, are
known for their poverty.
But their poverty is material. Their spiritual life knows
no poverty.
The monk's robe, worn and mended, is testimony to
the world of his poverty.
His Zen, which no one sees, is treasure beyond all
value.
This jewel, rare and of incalculable value, never changes
however one uses it.
And others can freely benefit from it on all occasions.

12

The three bodies* and the four knowledges** are perfect in this treasure.
The eight emancipations*** and the six supernatural powers**** are impressed upon it.

* The body of law and illumination, our normal body; the body of transformation, the individuality of an enlightened disciple; the body of spiritual bliss.

** Wisdom like a mirror which reflects perfectly without being affected itself; the wisdom of equality, all-embracing compassion; the wisdom of difference which perceives things in their true reality; the wisdom by which actions succeed.

*** Emancipation by entry into a subtle form; by entry into non-form; by purity; by entry into the region of infinite space; by entry into the region of infinite awareness; by entry into the region of 'nothing is'; by entry into the region of 'neither perception nor non-perception'; total emancipation after the knowledge of annihilation.

**** The power of the eye of Devas which enables the appearance and disappearance of beings to be seen; the power of hearing human or divine sounds, near or far-away; the power to know others' psyches; the power to know their previous existence; the power to become multiple from being one, to walk on water and so on; the knowledge of the extinction of the abcesses of desire, enmity and ignorance.

13

By Za Zen we can obtain these eight emancipations and these six powers.

Students in Zen of the highest class (*Joshi*) pass directly to the ultimate truth.

Those of the middle class (*Chushi*) and of the lower class (*Geshi*) like to teach others but have no deep convictions themselves.

Once you have revealed your prejudices you can see your true self.

How can you wander off into external struggles?

14

Some men pour scorn on Zen or hold it in question.
They play with fire, trying in vain to burn the sky.
A true student of Zen should hear what they
say as if their words were sweet drops of dew,
Forgetting even their sweetness however when he
enters into the realm of the non-mental.
I consider hurtful words as virtuous actions
And I treat those who hurt me as good masters,
For I feel neither for nor against the man who insults
me.
I do not need to explain the two powers of perseverance,
the understanding of without-birth and without-death,
suchness, Nirvana.

15

It is necessary to reach true Zen and to acquire eloquence in instruction.
Za Zen and wisdom should shine forth without being dimmed by any idea of vacuity.
Such accomplishment is not restricted to a few.
The Buddhas, as numberless as the sands of the Ganges, all bear witness to this fact.

16

The fearless thought of Zen is like the powerful roaring of a lion,
Striking terror into the hearts of all other animals.
Even the king of the elephants runs off, forgetting his dignity.
Students of good heart, they alone, like the old dragon hear that roaring with calm delight.

17

Students of Zen travel by land and sea, crossing rivers
and mountains,
Visiting monasteries and receiving instruction from the
Masters in person.
I too followed this way, reaching Sokei where I found
my Master and received Dharma.
Now I know that my true being has nothing to do with
birth and death.
A student in Zen walks in Zen and sits in Zen.
Whether he speaks or acts, whether he is silent or
inactive, his body is always peaceful.
He smiles, looking straight at the word which takes his
life.
He keeps his balance even at the moment of death and
no drug can disturb his calmness.

18

Our great Master Sakyamuni met the Buddha Dipankara millions of years ago and received his Dharma.
Since then he has been Master of patience, life after life.
Man is born several times, and he dies several times.
Life and death follow on one another unceasingly.
If he realizes the true meaning of non-birth, a man transcends riches and honours.
He lives alone in the mountain and the deep valleys,
He practises Za Zen under the old pine trees, in comfort.
He lives quietly and simply.

19

Those who understand always act naturally.
Most men live in impermanence, the unreal, but students
of Zen live in the real.
Those who give without the spirit of perfect giving,
which wants no result, will go to heaven for a short
time and return.
They direct arrows against the sky.
The arrow shot at the sky falls to earth.
When effort and reward are equal, nothing remains.
Effort without goal is quite different.

20

He opens the door of truth which leads to the garden of
Tathagata.
A true student of Zen ignores the branches and the
leaves, and aims for the root.
Like the image of the moon reflected in a jade bowl
I know the true beauty of the jewel of freedom,
For myself and for others.

21

The moon rises above the river
On the bank the wind plays softly in the pines
all night long, pure and calm.
What is the meaning of that serenity?
Look on the Buddha's precepts of nature.
Winter and autumn mists, dew, clouds, spring mists
are the true robe which covers our body.

22

Once a begging bowl vanquished dragons* and a stick
pacified tigers fighting.**
The staff has six rings at the top, their jingling awakens
people from dreams.
The bowl and staff are not mere symbols of instruction
But the action of Tathagata in the world.

* The tale is told of a drought in ancient China. In order to
obtain rain some monks read the Dragon Sutra, hoping to call
down the sky dragon who was responsible for drought. The
dragon came into one of the monks' bowls and then the rain
came pelting down.

** One day Master Chou saw two tigers in fierce combat. He put
his staff between them and instantly they stopped fighting.

The bowl and staff are the spirit and nature of Buddha which
enables us to move mountains.

23

It is not necessary to look for truth or avoid illusion.
We know that both are comprised in Ku, emptiness,
that they have no form and bounds.
Non-form is neither empty nor non-empty.
It is the true reality of Buddha.

24

Our spirit is like a clear mirror
Thus it reflects the universe harmoniously
Our spirit and the universe are one.

25

All that the universe contains, its many forms,
are reflected by the spirit
which shines like a perfect jewel without surface or interior.
The void, defined negatively, refutes causality.
Then everything is in complete confusion, without order.
All manner of troubles arise if we abandon *U* (existence) to obtain *Ku* (emptiness); that too is sickness.
It is like throwing oneself into the fire to escape drowning.

26

If we try to grasp truth or if we wish to escape error and illusion, we practise discrimination, an artificial and erroneous attitude.
When a practitioner of Za Zen does not understand his spirit he should use a little asceticism.
Then he is ready to see the thief as his own dear son.

27

Most men forget spirit treasure, lose their own merit
and dishonour Buddhism as a whole.
They have recourse to dualist thinking and abandon
the true nature of spirit.
To pass the barrier of Zen by means of Za Zen,
we should finish with reason, knowledge, illusion.
Then we shall attain to supreme wisdom and enter into
the palace of Nirvana (*Satori*).

32

There is one Nature, perfect and penetrative, present in all natures;
One Reality which includes all, comprising all realities in itself.
The one moon is reflected wherever there is water.
And all moons in water are comprised in the one moon.

39

The Spirit operates naturally through the organs of
sense.
Thus the objective world is perceived.
This dualism mists the mirror.
But when the haze is removed, the light shines forth.
Thus when each individual spirit and the objective
world are forgotten and emptied suchness affirms Truth.

54

Vision is clear.
But there are no objects to see.
There is no person.
There is no Buddha.

The void smiles

It comes only in true awakening.
Fools strive after sanctity,
Or for rewards.
The stone lantern lifts its hand:
Daybreak is here.
The void smiles and
Nods its great head.

Nensho

Blossom

Blossom seizes my spirit.
How?
I have long since withdrawn from the world
and all that is worldly.
All things are one to me.
How then does blossom make me rejoice?

Saigyo

94

Life and death

Suddenly light
Suddenly dark —
I am firefly too.

Chinejo

Lanterns

The moon sinks
Behind the mountain.
Across the wide watery darkness
Fishing-lights wink.
We think we are alone but
Far out there on the midnight sea
Oars are splashing
A long way out,
Further out than us.

Manyoshu

Life and death

While living, identify with life; when dying, with death.
Do not give way, do not desire. Life and death are the
essential being of Buddha. If therefore you abandon
life and death you will lose; and if you attach yourself
either to life or to death, you will lose. Do not hate and
do not desire; do not think and do not speak of these
things. Forget your body and spirit and put them in
the Buddha's hands and let him guide you. Then without striving for an end you will reach freedom and
Buddhahood. The way there is easy. Shun evil, do nothing
about life and death, show mercy to all living things,
show respect to your superiors and sympathy to your
inferiors. Do not like or dislike. Live without worry or
speculation. That is the only way to Buddhahood.

Dogen

Self-portrait

I am too old and too lazy to write poems.
Age seems to be my only loyal friend now.
In some life long ago I was (unfortunately) a poet.
Perhaps I was a painter (or some sort of painter) too.
As is customary, the world remembers me
For this or that movement of my hand.
My name is known because this hand moved thus.
But the real me, ah! that they
cannot reach.

Wang Wei

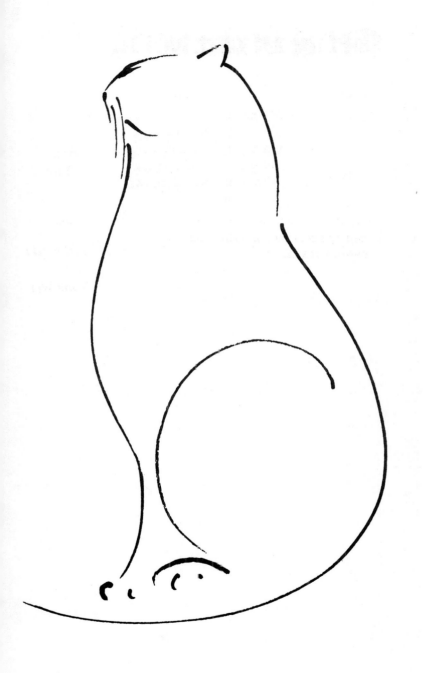

Being in the world

My existence —
The moon shining
On a drop of water
On the palm of a hand.
Who in the world knows
If it is there
Or not?

Ki No Tsurayuki

I grow old

I grow old —
Sweet bird you vanish
into autumn twilight.

Basho

Eternity

I hereby leave and bequeath
In perpetuity
To this bird this fence.

Issa

Defiance

Do what you will, frost.
You cannot hurt me now —
I am the last chrysanthemum!

Oemaru

A white chrysanthemum
A perfect flower —
Scissors waver.

Buson

The Hannya Shingyo or Heart of True Wisdom

The Hannya Shingyo is the 'Great Song of the Heart of Wisdom', a hymn of true wisdom which is recited daily in Zen cloisters and was translated in 649 AD from Sanskrit into Chinese by Sanzo Hoshi Genyo.

The Bodhisattva, called Kan Ji Zai,
who reached supreme wisdom,
understood that all things of this world, constituted
of five existential elements, have no substance.
He bore away all bitterness
and all suffering.
He spoke:
O Sariputra
all appearances in the world
all manifestations
are not distinct from non-substance.
There is no distinction between non-substance
and phenomena. This means too that all appearances of
the world are 'non-substance'.
That means that non-substance
includes all worldly phenomena.
The same applies
to senses, ideas, will, perception.
O Sariputra!
All things in the world
have the appearance of non-substance.
There is nothing that is born,
nothing that disappears.
There is neither impurity nor purity.

There is no growth
and no decrease of growth.
Therefore in non-substance
there are no appearances of this world.
There are no senses, ideas, will,
no perception.
There is no eye, no ear, no nose,
no tongue, no body, no brain.
No appearances of this world.
No voice, no smell, no taste,
nothing tangible.
No objects in the areas of sensual perception.
No field of vision, no realm of perception.
Nothing between the two.
There is no obstacle nor a disappearance
of obstacles.
No aging and no death.
There is no suffering and no cause of suffering.
There is no suppression of suffering
and no way of suppressing suffering.
There is no possibility of knowing and no
content of knowledge.
The Bodhisattvas pursue supreme wisdom.
For them there is no veil before the heart.
There is no veil and therefore there is no
fear.
Any obstacle that prevents them
from seeing clearly is behind them.
In the end they enter into Nirvana.
The Buddhas in the three worlds,
Past, present and future,
have attained to the best, the supreme Satori,
for they pursued supreme wisdom.
Therefore we must come to know
perfect wisdom.

That is the great word of dedication.
It is the great mantra of wisdom
It is the highest word.
It is the incomparable word of dedication
which wholly banishes suffering.
Truly, truly
the word which reveals perfect wisdom
is this:
O all who go
O all who go in perfection
O men who go to Nirvana
Alleluia!
O Satori, alleluia!